BEAUTIFUL ANIME GIRLS

COLORING BOOK
FOR KIDS

This book belongs to

____

Author: Charlie S. McTony

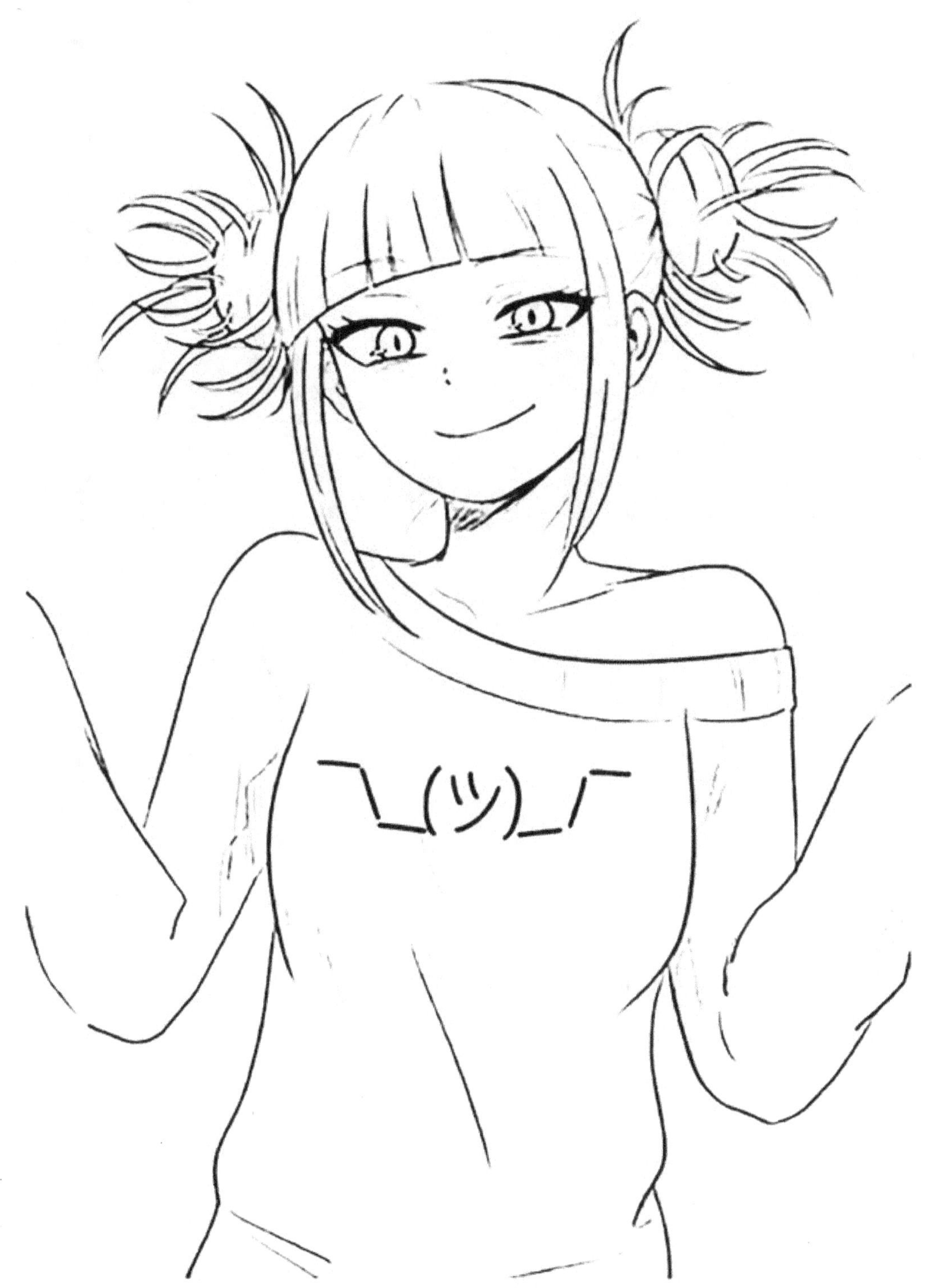
¯_(ツ)_/¯

Thank you.

We hope you enjoyed our book.

As a small family company, your feedback is
very important to us.

Please let us know how you like our book at:
adrian.stoica@deannaosc.com